I0514024

"In this world nothing can be said to be certain, except death and taxes."

-Benjamin Franklin

While many dread the April 15th tax deadline each year…. pulling together information for the accountant, requesting lost tax documents from employers, gathering receipts for business purchases… many tax professionals, including me, thrive on tax season. The ability to help taxpayers save as much as possible on their return, helping taxpayers become compliant with past filings (to date, my record is preparing nine years of tax returns for a taxpayer), or responding to IRS notices, drives me. The adrenaline flow that comes when a client brings in boxes of files to sort; all at a cost, of course.
If you pass by my office (I work from home), you'll see a light on in the early morning hours as my mind races, thinking how I can work or rework a scenario on a tax return that will be in the best interest of the taxpayer. I grab a cup of coffee and begin the tasks of the day.

Taxpayers have varied ideas about preparing their taxes and who prepares them. Few realize what goes on behind the scenes to make the tax preparation business run. There is office staff training, continuing education, upgrades to software, unlimited phone calls and questions from clients, hours on the phone with the IRS, responding to IRS notices………

Recently, my wife read an online blog about someone who self-published a book on a particular topic. My mind began to race. I decided I wanted to publish a book, a simple book, a primer style of do's and don'ts when filing your tax return. This book is a result of that inspiration. Some pages will make you laugh. Some will make you shake your head. Some will make you wonder.

I hope you enjoy.

is for

Always

Always open all correspondence from the IRS. The problem only gets worse when you don't.

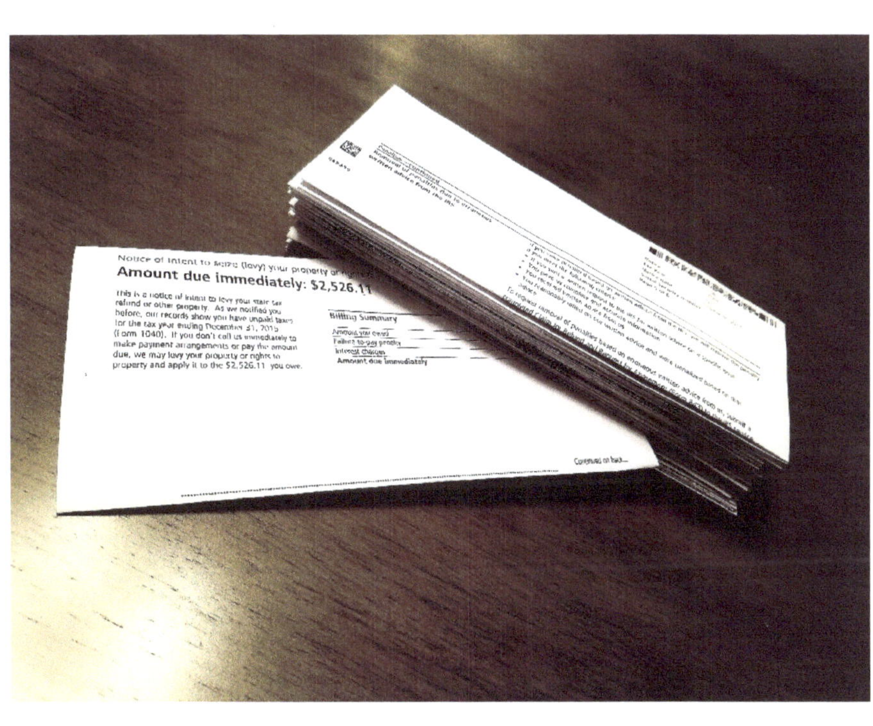
Amount due immediately: $2,526.11
Billing Summary
Amount due immediately
Continued on back...

B

is for

Be

Be on time to have your taxes prepared.

Be respectful. Your preparer's time is valuable during tax season.

MADE BY THE SESSIONS CLOCK CO., FORESTVILLE, CONN. U.S.A.

C

is for

Check

Check your paystubs periodically to ensure you have sufficient federal withholdings so you're not surprised with a balance due when you file your tax return.

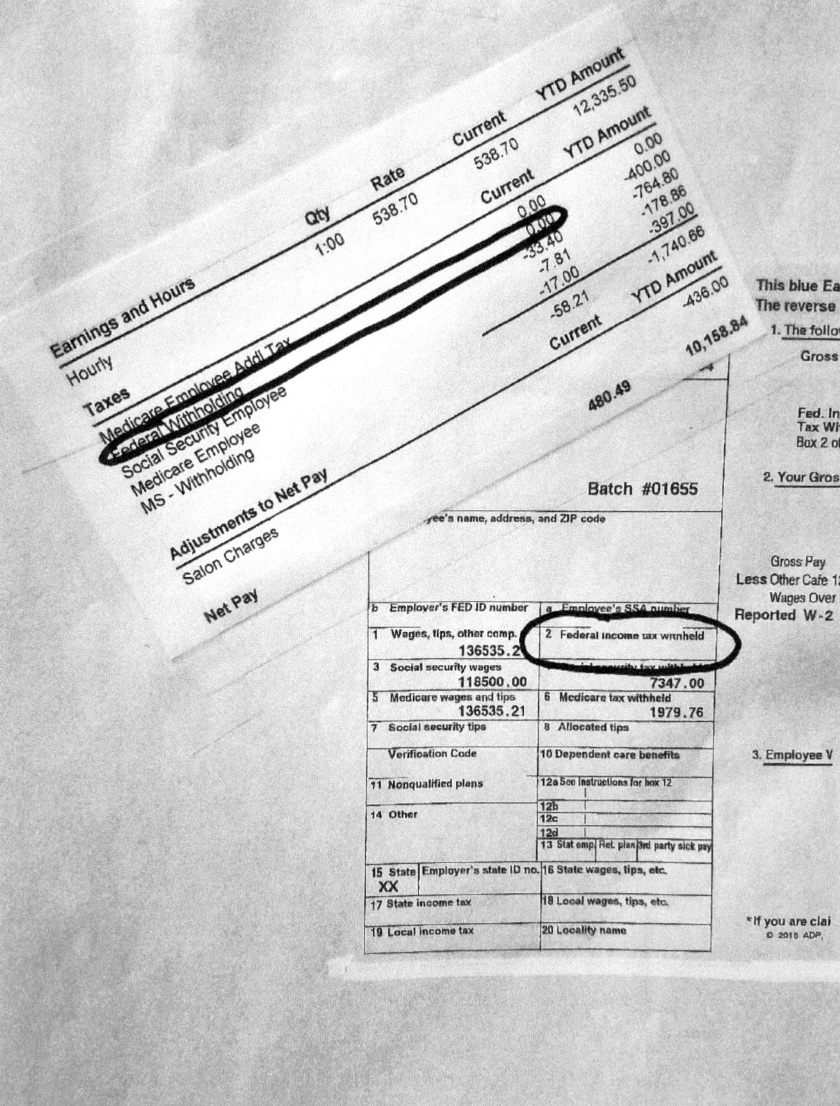

Earnings and Hours	Qty	Rate	Current	YTD Amount
Hourly	1:00	538.70	538.70	12,335.50

Taxes	Current	YTD Amount
Medicare Employee Addl Tax	0.00	0.00
Federal Withholding	0.00	-400.00
Social Security Employee	-33.40	-764.80
Medicare Employee	-7.81	-178.86
MS - Withholding	-17.00	-397.00
	-58.21	-1,740.66

Adjustments to Net Pay	Current	YTD Amount
Salon Charges		-436.00
Net Pay	480.49	10,158.84

Batch #01655

...yee's name, address, and ZIP code	
b Employer's FED ID number	a Employee's SSA number
1 Wages, tips, other comp. 136535.2	2 Federal income tax withheld
3 Social security wages 118500.00	7347.00
5 Medicare wages and tips 136535.21	6 Medicare tax withheld 1979.76
7 Social security tips	8 Allocated tips
Verification Code	10 Dependent care benefits
11 Nonqualified plans	12a See instructions for box 12
14 Other	12b
	12c
	12d
	13 Stat emp. Ret. plan 3rd party sick pay
15 State XX Employer's state ID no.	16 State wages, tips, etc.
17 State income tax	18 Local wages, tips, etc.
19 Local income tax	20 Locality name

This blue Earn

The reverse si

1. The followi

Gross P

Fed. Inco

Tax With

Box 2 of W

2. Your Gross

Gross Pay

Less Other Cafe 12

Wages Over I

Reported W-2

3. Employee V

*If you are clai

© 2016 ADP,

D

is for

Don't

Don't make excuses for not filing your tax return on time.

"I couldn't file my tax return because the pig ate my W-2."

W-2

E

is for

Everyone

Everyone will give you tax advice.
Family. Friends. Neighbors.
Cashiers.

Get knowledgeable advice from a
tax professional.

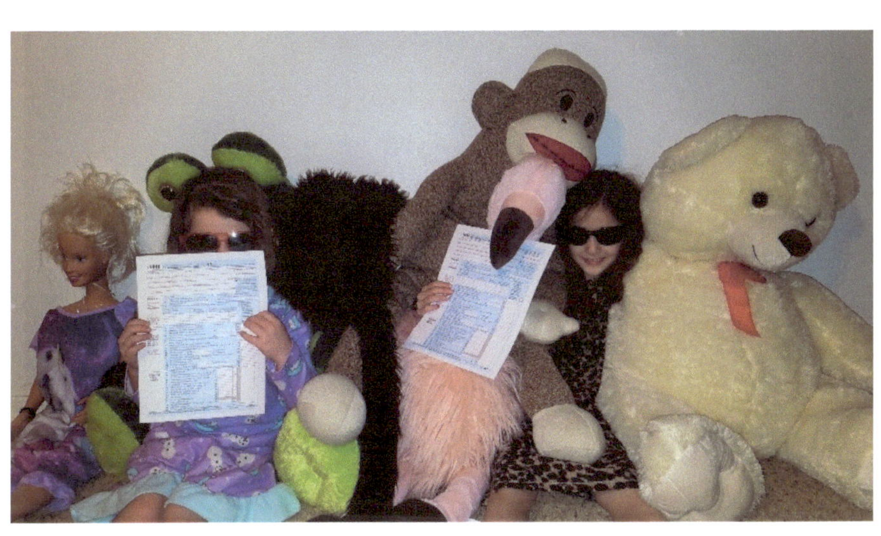

F

is for

Free

Free tax returns are not always your best option. Often returns done by family or friends don't take advantage of potential tax savings.

Remember, you usually get what you pay for.

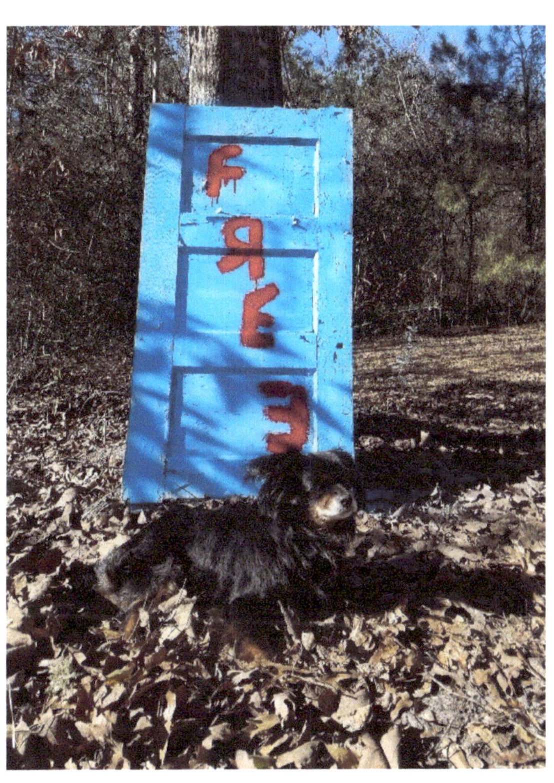
FREE

G

is for

Give

Give your tax professional ample time to prepare your return. You want the best outcome possible.

Understand that your tax professional needs time to review and verify your information and may not prepare a tax return while you wait. You want accuracy, not speed.

FREE

G

is for

Give

Give your tax professional ample time to prepare your return. You want the best outcome possible.

Understand that your tax professional needs time to review and verify your information and may not prepare a tax return while you wait. You want accuracy, not speed.

Return
1545-0008
ress, and ZIP code
ANCE CO OF AMER
- PREMIUM ACCOU
her comp.
5,960.67
tax withheld
1,005.05
wages
5,960.67
ithheld
250.35
86.43
Dependent care benefits
tips, etc.
5,960.67
tax
211670
X

H

is for

How

"How can I owe that much?! Do you realize how many deductions I have taken out of each paycheck?!"

(See *C is for Check.*)

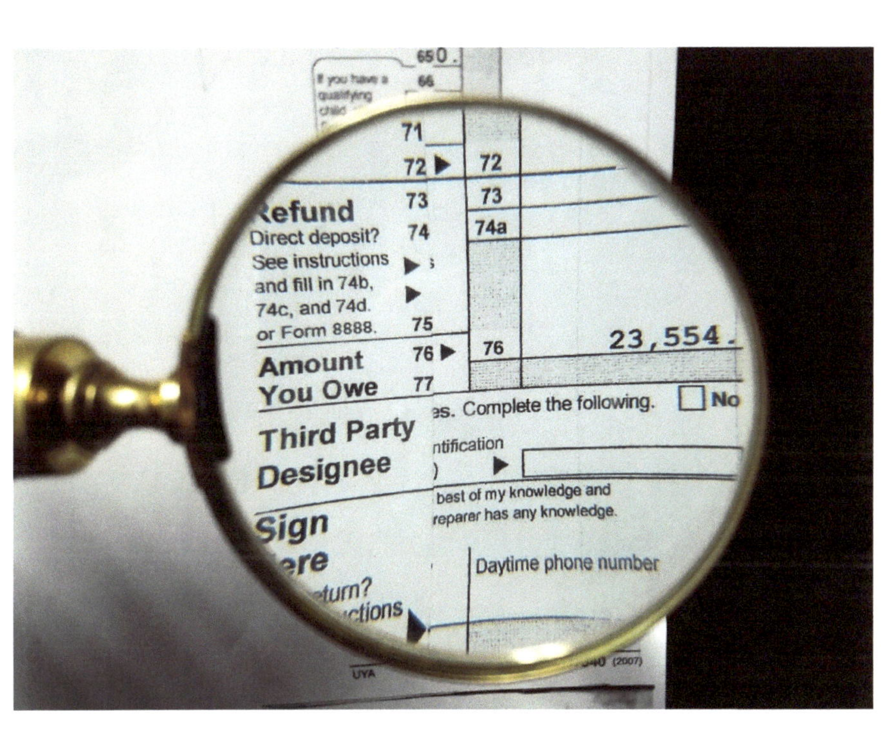

Refund
Direct deposit?
See instructions
and fill in 74b,
74c, and 74d.
or Form 8888.
Amount
You Owe
Third Party
Designee
Sign
es. Complete the following.
No
ntification
best of my knowledge and
reparer has any knowledge.
Daytime phone number
23,554.

I

is for

I

"I planned to pay my tax preparer for his services with my refund, but something came up."

Remember, your preparer has obligations too, including the cost of tax software, continuing education, and office supplies used to prepare the return.

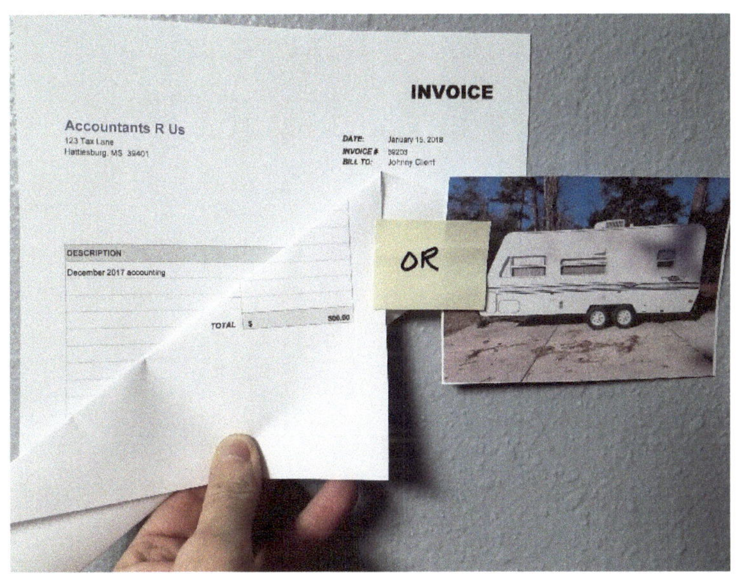
INVOICE
Accountants R Us
123 Tax Lane
Hattiesburg, MS 39401
DATE: January 15, 2018
INVOICE #
BILL TO: Johnny Client
DESCRIPTION
December 2017 accounting
TOTAL $
OR

J

is for

Just

Just because your friend or neighbor gets a large refund by using a particular tax professional doesn't mean you will.

No two clients have the same tax scenario.

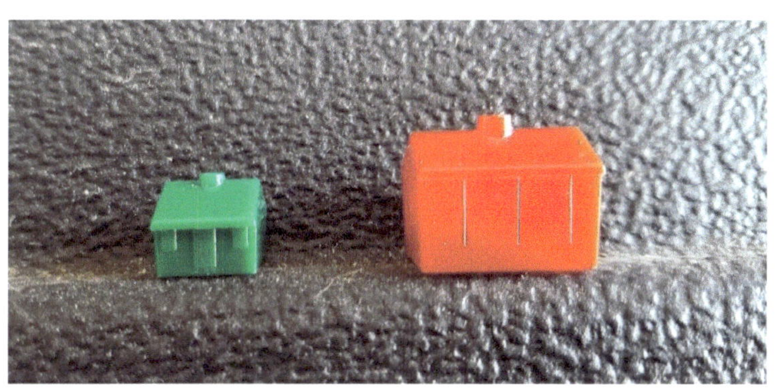

K

is for

Know

Know your filing status. Don't let an online refund calculator determine it for you.

Many factors are involved, such as the amount of support provided to an individual and the amount of time you lived with your spouse.

L

is for

Let

Let your tax professional tell you how the information you provide will be reported on the tax return, not the other way around.

After all, there's a reason you came to him or her in the first place.

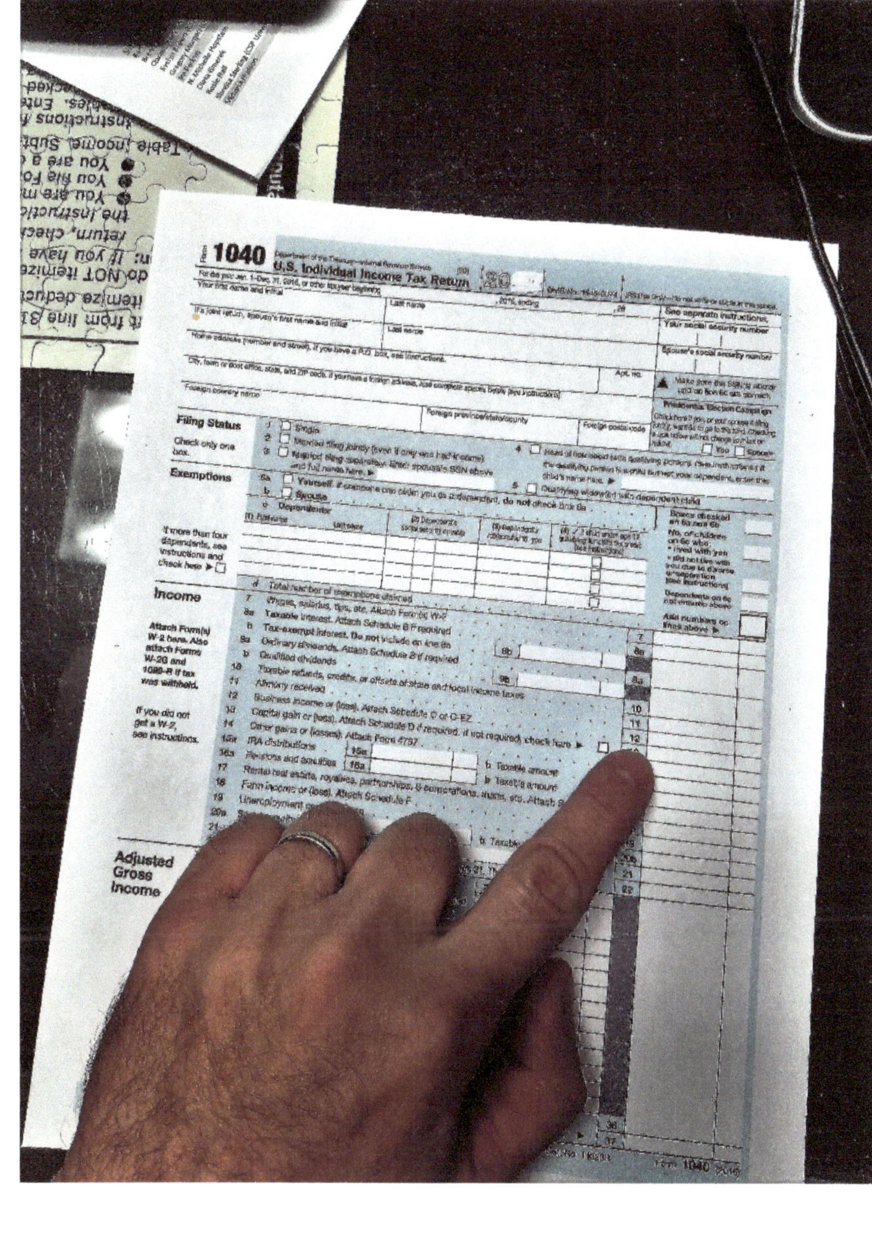

1040
U.S. Individual Income Tax Return
Filing Status
Check only one box.
Exemptions
If more than four dependents, see instructions and check here ▶
Income
Attach Form(s) W-2 here. Also attach Forms W-2G and 1099-R if tax was withheld.
If you did not get a W-2, see instructions.
Adjusted Gross Income

M

is for

Make

Make sure you have ALL your tax documents in hand before making an appointment.

Filing too early could result in you having to file an amended return later. Arriving at an appointment without all tax documents is wasted time for you and your tax professional.

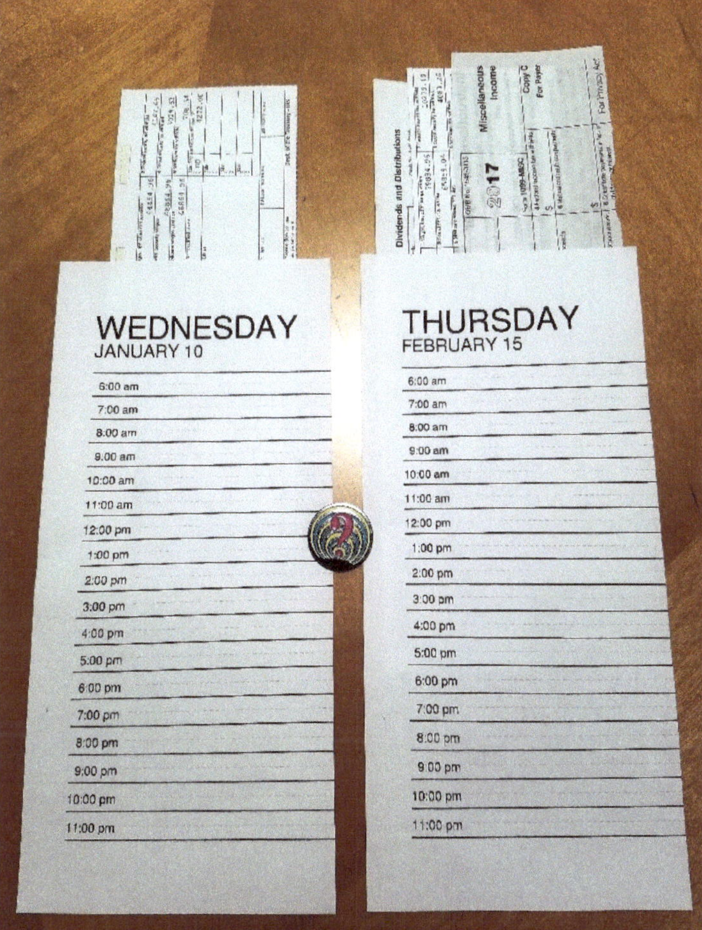

WEDNESDAY
JANUARY 10
6:00 am
7:00 am
8:00 am
9:00 am
10:00 am
11:00 am
12:00 pm
1:00 pm
2:00 pm
3:00 pm
4:00 pm
5:00 pm
6:00 pm
7:00 pm
8:00 pm
9:00 pm
10:00 pm
11:00 pm
THURSDAY
FEBRUARY 15
6:00 am
7:00 am
8:00 am
9:00 am
10:00 am
11:00 am
12:00 pm
1:00 pm
2:00 pm
3:00 pm
4:00 pm
5:00 pm
6:00 pm
7:00 pm
8:00 pm
9:00 pm
10:00 pm
11:00 pm
Dividends and Distributions
Miscellaneous Income
Copy C
For Payer
2017

N

is for

Never

Never claim someone on your tax return who is not your dependent.

Waiting For Network

Now...go enjoy your birthday!

n thank you!!

FEB 4, 2016 AT 1:17 PM

Hey I have a tax question. It seems that our niece [redacted] won't be used in her parents taxes this year. Let me ask you a few questions please. If we were to use her on our taxes 1. Is it ethical? 2. Is it legal? 3. Will it affect us at all?

1:31 PM

O

is for Overwhelmed

Overwhelmed with paperwork when preparing your tax return?

Engage the services of a tax professional such as an enrolled agent or certified public accountant.

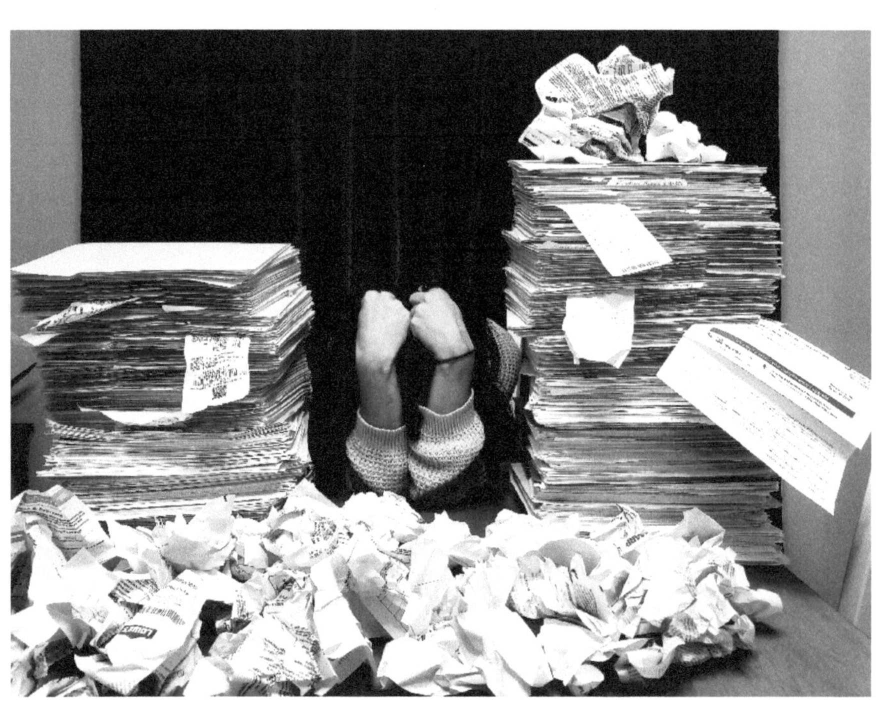

P

is for

Protect

Protect your identity at all cost. Always burn or shred any documents with identifying information such as your social security number. Thieves are always on the lookout for ways to steal your information.

Robbie Roberson
Tax Service
(601) 545-1634
Notary

Q

is for

Quickly

Quickly file an extension when you can't file a timely return.

Your tax professional will thank you for not calling at the last minute to file an extension or a tax return for you.

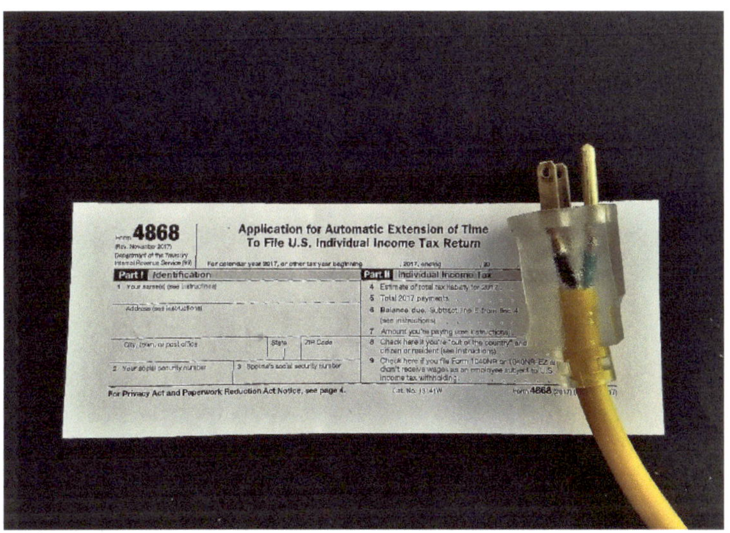
Form 4868
Application for Automatic Extension of Time
To File U.S. Individual Income Tax Return
Part I Identification
Part II Individual Income Tax
For Privacy Act and Paperwork Reduction Act Notice, see page 4.

R

is for

Read

Read the fine print on the bottom of the 1040 before you sign the return.

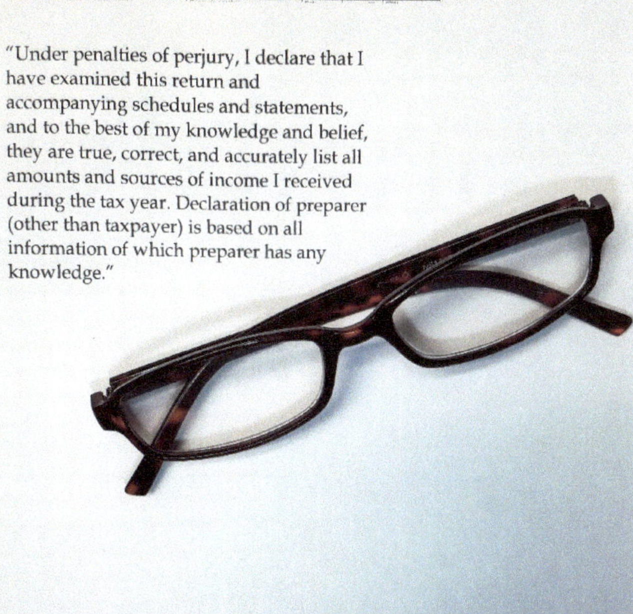
Sign here
Joint return? See instructions. Keep a copy for your records.
"Under penalties of perjury, I declare that I have examined this return and accompanying schedules and statements, and to the best of my knowledge and belief, they are true, correct, and accurately list all amounts and sources of income I received during the tax year. Declaration of preparer (other than taxpayer) is based on all information of which preparer has any knowledge."

S

is for

Supply

Supply your tax professional with only the information needed to prepare your return.

Tax professionals don't need to see receipts for your traffic tickets, dog vaccinations, or grocery lists.

bread
milk
bath soap
drinks
crackers
FORM SSA-1099 –
2017
中国人民银行
1
壹圆
SA24419607
Simply Fashion
Celebrating 20 Years
preferred guest
extra

T

is for

Tell

Tell your tax professional about any dealings you've had with the IRS in the past.

Don't let him have to find out from the IRS that you have a federal lien filed against you or your account is currently in collections.

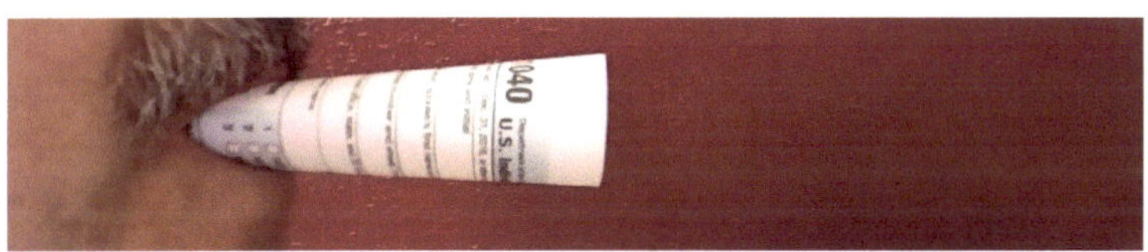

U

is for

Update

Update all life changes in the past year with your tax professional.

These include marriage, divorce, and/or a new child.

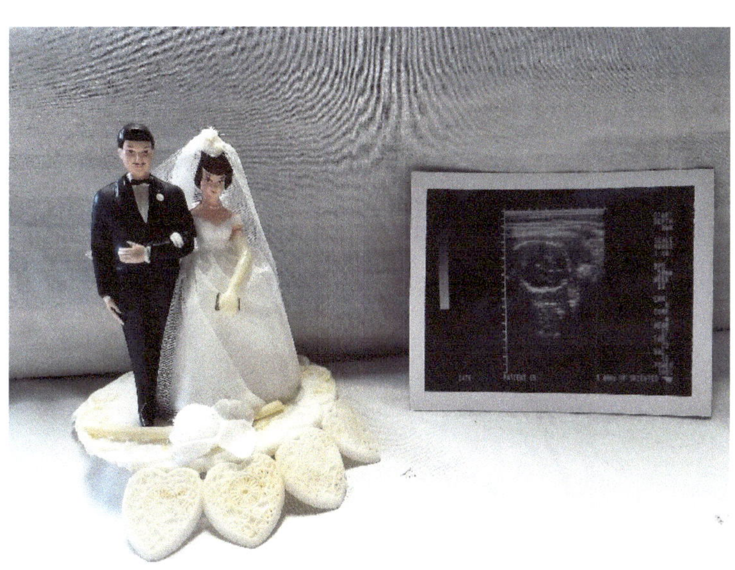

V

is for

Verify

Verify that the person whom you paid to prepare your tax return signed your tax return as the paid preparer.

Some tax offices appear from January 1-April 15, then close their doors, never to be seen again.

Anyone who prepares a return for a fee and doesn't sign the return is subject to a penalty.

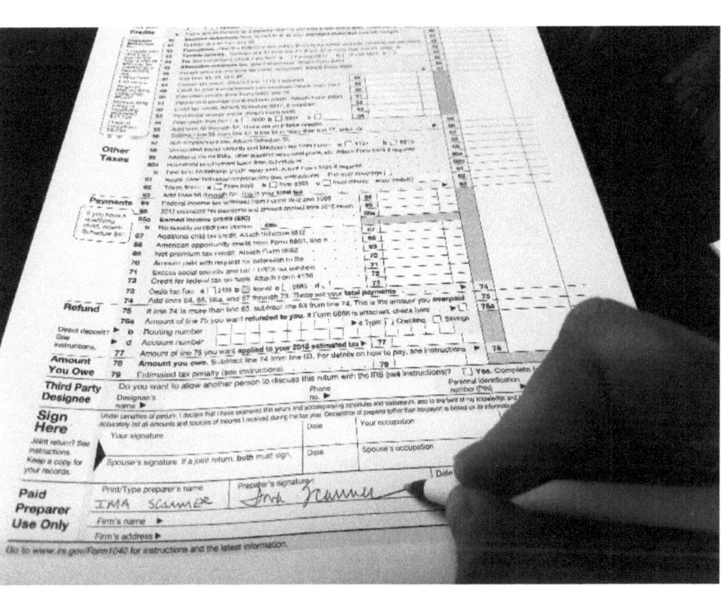
Other Taxes
Payments
Refund
Routing number
Account number
Amount You Owe
Amount you owe.
Third Party Designee
Do you want to allow another person to discuss this return with the IRS (see instructions)?
Sign Here
Your signature
Your occupation
Spouse's occupation
Paid Preparer Use Only
Print/Type preparer's name
Preparer's signature
IMA SCAMMER
Firm's name ▶
Firm's address ▶
Go to www.irs.gov/Form1040 for instructions and the latest information.

W

is for

Why

Why not save receipts throughout the year, such as medical bills, cash donations to a non-profit organization, and material goods given to a thrift store?

These receipts could help you itemize and give you a few extra dollars on your refund check (or even decrease your balance due).

is for

Xerox

Xeroxed or scanned documents can often be used as well as originals when preparing your return.

However, don't bring an old flash drive loaded with your tax information. A used flash drive may contain a virus, and many tax professionals won't accept them.

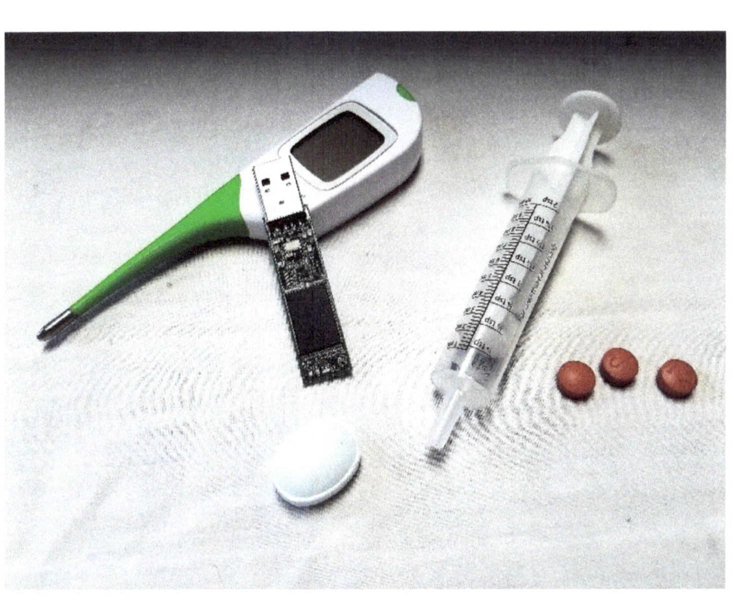

Y

is for

You

You are ultimately responsible for any, and all information reported on your tax return.

Be open, honest, and forthcoming with all information when meeting your tax professional.

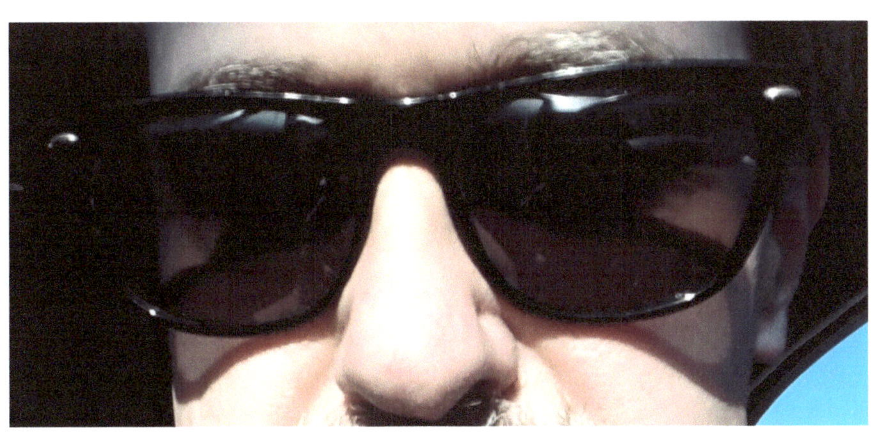

Z

is for

Zero

Zero in on things that will make preparing your return easier for your tax professional. Having your documents well notated and in order will help the process go more smoothly and will take less time; possibly resulting in lower preparation fees.

Tax

Afterword

Thank you for taking the time to purchase this book and read it. I hope you enjoyed a few "Aha" or "That sounds just like ________ " moments.

As an accountant I enjoy my work immensely. I enjoy meeting the demands of the day and meeting new clients with new stories each tax season.

If you are my client or a client of another tax professional, thank you for your business and the referrals you send our way.

If you are a tax professional, thank you for your dedication and time devoted to your clients.

As for thank you's, I would like to give a GIANT thank you to my wife, Thelma, who has stood by me for the past 21 tax seasons. After retirement in 2015, she joined me in my practice and takes a huge load off me by fielding phone calls, and taking on any task I send her way. She helps keep me focused and motivated. I couldn't make it without her.

Biography

Robbie Roberson, E.A., is an enrolled agent from Hattiesburg, MS. He began his accounting practice in 1998.

He published the article "A Closer Look Inside Publication 17: Beyond the Basics" in EA Journal in 2014. He served as editor of EA Journal in 2016.

Robbie is a member of National Society of Enrolled Agents and Mississippi Society of Enrolled Agents. As of this printing, Robbie serves as Secretary of MSSEA as well as the social media coordinator.

In his spare time, Robbie enjoys traveling, photography, and geocaching.

What is an Enrolled Agent?

An enrolled agent is a person who has earned the privilege of representing taxpayers before the Internal Revenue Service by either passing a three-part comprehensive IRS test covering individual and business tax returns, or through experience as a former IRS employee. Enrolled agent status is the highest credential the IRS awards. Individuals who obtain this elite status must adhere to ethical standards and complete 72 hours of continuing education courses every three years.

Enrolled agents, like attorneys and certified public accountants (CPAs), have unlimited practice rights. This means they are unrestricted as to which taxpayers they can represent, what types of tax matters they can handle, and which IRS offices they can represent clients before. Learn more about enrolled agents in Treasury Department Circular 230 (PDF).

You can easily locate an enrolled agent in your area by visiting the "Find a Tax Expert" website taxexperts.naea.org and searching by location or specialty. You might also want to check in your local yellow pages under "Tax Preparation," and look for the phrase "Enrolled Agent," "Enrolled to Represent Taxpayers before the IRS," or the EA credential following the professional's name.

1040 Lagniappe

On the 2017 Form 1040,

The word 'income' appears 15 times.

The word 'tax' appears 38 times (in some form).

The word 'schedule' appears 14 times.

The word 'dependent' appears nine times.

The word 'child' appears nine times.

The number '1040' appears five times. (Look closely or you might miss some of them.)

The word 'gain' appears only two times, while....

The word 'loss' appears four times.

But the word 'refund' appears four times, while....

The word 'owe' only appears only two times.

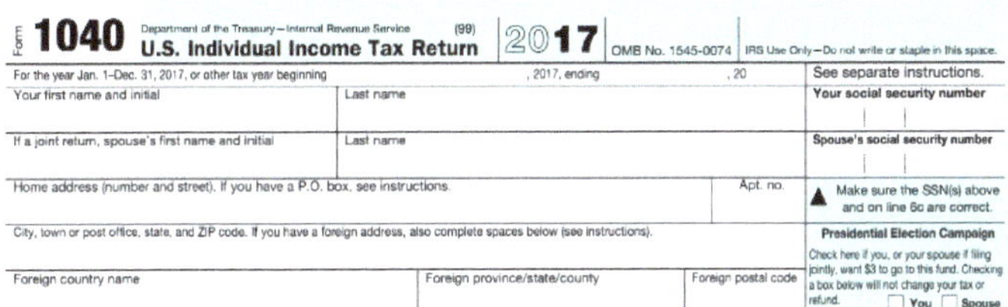

Form **1040** Department of the Treasury—Internal Revenue Service (99)
U.S. Individual Income Tax Return **2017** OMB No. 1545-0074 IRS Use Only—Do not write or staple in this space.

For the year Jan. 1–Dec. 31, 2017, or other tax year beginning , 2017, ending , 20 | See separate instructions.

Your first name and initial | Last name | **Your social security number**

If a joint return, spouse's first name and initial | Last name | **Spouse's social security number**

Home address (number and street). If you have a P.O. box, see instructions. | Apt. no. | ▲ Make sure the SSN(s) above and on line 6c are correct.

City, town or post office, state, and ZIP code. If you have a foreign address, also complete spaces below (see instructions). | **Presidential Election Campaign**

Foreign country name | Foreign province/state/county | Foreign postal code | Check here if you, or your spouse if filing jointly, want $3 to go to this fund. Checking a box below will not change your tax or refund. ☐ **You** ☐ **Spouse**

Form 1040 Through the Years

TO BE FILLED IN BY COLLECTOR.

List. No. ....

.... District of ....

Date received ....

Form 1040.

INCOME TAX.

THE PENALTY
FOR FAILURE TO HAVE THIS RETURN IN THE HANDS OF THE COLLECTOR OF INTERNAL REVENUE ON OR BEFORE MARCH 1 IS $20 TO $1,000.
(SEE INSTRUCTIONS ON PAGE 4.)

TO BE FILLED IN BY INTERNAL REVENUE BUREAU.

File No. ....

Assessment List ....

Page .... Line ....

UNITED STATES INTERNAL REVENUE.

RETURN OF ANNUAL NET INCOME OF INDIVIDUALS.

(As provided by Act of Congress, approved October 3, 1913.)

RETURN OF NET INCOME RECEIVED OR ACCRUED DURING THE YEAR ENDED DECEMBER 31, 191 ....

(FOR THE YEAR 1913, FROM MARCH 1, TO DECEMBER 31.)

Filed by (or for) .... of ....
(Full name of individual.) (Street and No.)

in the City, Town, or Post Office of .... State of ....
(Fill in pages 2 and 3 before making entries below.)

1. GROSS INCOME (see page 2, line 12)		$
2. GENERAL DEDUCTIONS (see page 3, line 7)		$
3. NET INCOME		$
Deductions and exemptions allowed in computing income subject to the normal tax of 1 per cent.		
4. Dividends and net earnings received or accrued, of corporations, etc., subject to like tax. (See page 2, line 11)	$	
5. Amount of income on which the normal tax has been deducted and withheld at the source. (See page 2, line 9, column A)		
6. Specific exemption of $3,000 or $4,000, as the case may be. (See Instructions 3 and 19)		
Total deductions and exemptions. (Items 4, 5, and 6)		$
7. TAXABLE INCOME on which the normal tax of 1 per cent is to be calculated. (See Instruction 3)		$

8. When the net income shown above on line 3 exceeds $20,000, the additional tax thereon must be calculated as per schedule below:

	INCOME.	TAX.
1 per cent on amount over $20,000 and not exceeding $50,000	$	$
2 " " 50,000 " " 75,000		
3 " " 75,000 " " 100,000		
4 " " 100,000 " " 250,000		
5 " " 250,000 " " 500,000		
6 " " 500,000		
Total additional or super tax		$
Total normal tax (1 per cent of amount entered on line 7)		$
Total tax liability		$

IF RETURN IS FOR CALENDAR YEAR 1920 FILE IT WITH THE COLLECTOR OF INTERNAL REVENUE FOR YOUR DISTRICT ON OR BEFORE MARCH 15, 1921

IF FOR A PERIOD OTHER THAN A CALENDAR YEAR THE RETURN SHOULD BE FILED ON OR BEFORE THE 15TH DAY OF THE THIRD MONTH FOLLOWING THE CLOSE OF SUCH PERIOD

Form 1040—UNITED STATES INTERNAL REVENUE SERVICE

INDIVIDUAL INCOME TAX RETURN

FOR NET INCOMES OF MORE THAN $5,000 OR SEPARATE RETURNS OF HUSBAND AND WIFE IF COMBINED NET INCOME EXCEEDS $5,000

FOR CALENDAR YEAR 1920

Or for period begun ...., 19......, and ended ...., 19......

If the return is made for a period other than a calendar year, the dates of the beginning and ending of the period covered must be plainly stated in the space provided above.

PRINT PLAINLY NAME, STREET AND NUMBER, OR RURAL ROUTE, POST OFFICE, COUNTY, AND STATE

Cash	
Check	
M. O.	
Cert. of Ind.	

(DO NOT WRITE IN THIS SPACE)

Examined by ....

Audited by ....

FIRST PAYMENT

$..........

Cashier's Stamp

I swear (or affirm) that this return, including the accompanying schedules and statements (if any), has been examined by me, and, to the best of my knowledge and belief, is a true and complete return made in good faith, for the taxable period as stated, pursuant to the Revenue Act of 1918 and the Regulations issued under authority thereof.

(If return is made by agent, the reason therefor must be stated on this line.)

Sworn to and subscribed before me this .... day of ...., 1921.

(Signature of individual or agent.)

(Signature of officer administering oath.) Title (Address of individual or agent.)

1. Are you a citizen of the United States? ....
2. If not, are you a resident of the United States? ....
3. If neither, of what country are you a citizen or subject? ....
4. Did you file a return for 1919? ....
5. If so, what address did you give on that return? ....
6. To what Collector's office was it sent? (Give district or city and State) ....
7. Did you receive any adjustments during the taxable period on account of a government contract through the purchase of a claims board or otherwise? ....
8. Were you married and living with wife (or husband) on the last day of your taxable period? ....
9. If not, were you on the last day of your taxable period supporting one or more persons living in your household who are closely related to you by blood, marriage, or adoption? ....
10. (a) How many dependent persons under 18 or if 18 or over, incapable of self support because mentally or physically defective) were receiving their chief support from you on the last day of your taxable period? ....
11. Was a separate return filed by your wife (or husband)? .... If so, state (a) exemption claimed $.......... (b) Name and address entered at head of that return ....
12. [illegible]
13. Did you pay during the calendar year 1920 to any individual rent, wages, salaries, or other fixed or determinable income amounting to $1,000 or over? .... (If so, secure from the Collector Forms 1096 and 1099 and file a return of information.)
14. Enter below all nontaxable income received by you during the taxable period from the following sources:

[illegible]

15. Enter in the table below (unless whether received or not) from partnerships, personal service corporations, and fiduciaries.

[illegible]

16. [illegible] Interest on Liberty Bonds and other obligations of the United States issued since September 1, 1917, and War Finance Corporation Bonds, received [illegible] (See page 3 of instructions, Schedule L.)

[illegible]

(k) Taxable interest ....

(l) Total taxable interest on all obligations as computed above on line (k) (enter as Item 19 below, and on Schedule L, page 2) .... $..........

State the amount of the Victory Liberty Loan 3¾% and 4¾% Notes originally subscribed for and still owned at the date of filing this return .... $..........

State the amount of the Fourth Liberty Loan 4¼% Bonds originally subscribed for and still owned at the date of filing this return .... $..........

COMPUTATION OF TAX.

17. Net income on which tax is to be computed (from Schedule D) .... $..........
18. Less: Dividends (from Schedule E) .... $..........
19. Taxable interest on Liberty Bonds, etc. (from Item 16 (l) above) ....
20. Personal exemption ....
21. Total of Items 18, 19, and 20 ....
22. Balance subject to normal tax (Item 17 minus Item 21) .... $..........
23. Amount subject to normal tax at 4% (not over $4,000) ....
24. Balance subject to normal tax at 8% (Item 22 minus Item 23) .... $..........
25. Normal tax at 4% on amount of Item 23 .... $..........
26. Normal tax at 8% on amount of Item 24 ....
27. Surtax on Item 17 (see surtax table, page 1 of instructions) ....
28. Total Tax .... $..........
29. Less: Tax paid at source .... $..........
30. Income and profits taxes paid during taxable period to foreign countries or possessions of the United States (attach Form 1116) .... $..........
31. Balance of tax due (Item 28 minus Items 29 and 30) ....
32. Amount of tax paid on submission of return .... $..........

PREPARATION OF RETURN.

Did you employ anyone especially to prepare or advise in the preparation of this return? (Answer "Yes" or "No") .... If so, give name and address and state the extent to which you received such assistance or advice ....

AMENDED RETURNS.

An amended return must be plainly marked "Amended" across the face of the return.

CHECKS AND DRAFTS.

Checks and drafts will be accepted only if payable at par at your Collector's office.

DETACH RETURN HERE AND SEND IT TO COLLECTOR OF INTERNAL REVENUE FOR YOUR DISTRICT.

INDIVIDUAL INCOME TAX RETURN

FOR NET INCOMES FROM SALARIES OR WAGES OF MORE THAN $5,000 AND INCOMES FROM BUSINESS, PROFESSION, RENTS, OR SALE OF PROPERTY

For Calendar Year 1930

File This Return With the Collector of Internal Revenue for Your District on or Before March 15, 1931

PRINT NAME AND ADDRESS PLAINLY BELOW

(Name)

(Street and number, or rural route)

(Post office) (County) (State)

Occupation

(Auditor's Stamp)

Do Not Write in These Spaces

File Code

Serial Number

District

(Cashier's Stamp)

Cash Check M. O. Cert. of Ind.

First Payment

$

1. Are you a citizen or resident of the United States?
2. If you filed a return for 1929, to what Collector's office was it sent?
3. Is this a joint return of husband and wife?
4. State name of husband or wife if a separate return was made and the Collector's office where it was sent
5. Were you married and living with husband or wife on the last day of your taxable year?
6. If not, were you on the last day of your taxable year supporting in your household one or more persons closely related to you?
7. If your status in respect to questions 5 and 6 changed during the year, state date and nature of change
8. How many dependent persons (other than husband or wife) under 18 years of age or incapable of self-support were receiving their chief support from you on the last day of your taxable year?

INCOME

Amount received — Expense paid (Explain in Schedule F)

1. Salaries, Wages, Commissions, etc. (State name and address of employer) $ $ $
2. Income from Business or Profession. (From Schedule A)
3. Interest on Bank Deposits, Notes, Corporation Bonds, etc. (except interest on tax-free covenant bonds)
4. Interest on Tax-free Covenant Bonds Upon Which a Tax was Paid at Source
5. Income from Partnerships. (State name and address)
6. Income from Fiduciaries. (State name and address)
7. Rents and Royalties. (From Schedule B)
8. Profit from Sale of Real Estate, Stocks, Bonds, etc. (From Schedule C)
9. Taxable Interest on Liberty Bonds, etc. (From Schedule E)
10. Dividends on Stock of Domestic Corporations
11. Other Income (including dividends on stock of foreign corporations). (State nature of income)
    (a)
    (b)
12. Total Income in Items 1 to 11 $

DEDUCTIONS

13. Interest Paid $
14. Taxes Paid. (Explain in Schedule F)
15. Losses by Fire, Storm, etc. (Explain in Table at foot of page 2)
16. Bad Debts. (Explain in Schedule F)
17. Contributions. (Explain in Schedule F)
18. Other Deductions Authorized by Law. (Explain in Schedule F)
19. Total Deductions in Items 13 to 18 $
20. Net Income (Item 12 minus Item 19) $

EARNED INCOME CREDIT

21. Earned Income (not over $30,000) $
22. Less Personal Exemption and Credit for Dependents
23. Balance (Item 21 minus 22) $
24. Amount taxable at 1½% (not over $4,000) $
25. Amount taxable at 3% (not over $4,000)
26. Amount taxable at 5% (balance over $8,000 of Item 23)
27. Normal Tax (1½% of Item 24) $
28. Normal Tax (3% of Item 25)
29. Normal Tax (5% of Item 26)
30. Surtax on Item 21
31. Tax on Earned Net Income (total of Items 27 to 30) $
32. Credit of 25% of Tax (not over 25% of Items 30, 44, 45, and 46) $

COMPUTATION OF TAX (See instruction 22)

33. Net Income (Item 20 above) $
    Less-
34. Liberty Bond Interest (Item 9) $
35. Dividends (Item 10)
36. Credit for Dependents
37. Personal Exemption
38. Total of Items 34 to 37
39. Balance (Item 33 minus 38) $
40. Amount taxable at 1½% (not over $4,000)
41. Balance (Item 39 minus 40) $
42. Amount taxable at 3% (not over $4,000)
43. Amount taxable at 5% (Item 41 minus 42) $
44. Normal Tax (1½% of Item 40) $
45. Normal Tax (3% of Item 42)
46. Normal Tax (5% of Item 43)
47. Surtax on Item 20 (see Instruction 23)
48. Tax on Net Income (total of Items 44 to 47) $
49. Tax on Capital Gain or Loss (12½% of Col. 8, Sched. D)
50. Total of or difference between Items 48 and 49 $
51. Less Credit of 25% of Tax on Earned Income (Item 32)
52. Total Tax (Item 50 minus 51) $
53. Less Income Tax Paid at Source
54. Income Tax paid to a foreign country or U. S. possession
55. Balance of Tax (Item 52 minus Items 53 and 54) $

AFFIDAVIT

I swear (or affirm) that this return, including the accompanying schedules and statements, has been examined by me, and to the best of my knowledge and belief, is a true and complete return made in good faith for the taxable year stated, pursuant to the Revenue Act of 1928 and the Regulations issued thereunder.

(If return is made by agent, the reason therefor must be stated on this line)

Sworn to and subscribed before me this ______ day of ____________, 1931. ____________ (Signature of individual or agent)

NOTARIAL SEAL ____________ (Signature of officer administering oath) ____________ (Title) ____________ (Address of agent)

An amended return must be marked "Amended" at top of return. Checks and drafts will be accepted only if payable at par

FORM 1040
Treasury Department
Internal Revenue Service

Page 1

UNITED STATES
INDIVIDUAL INCOME AND DEFENSE TAX RETURN

1940

(Auditor's Stamp)

FOR GROSS INCOMES OF MORE THAN $5,000 FROM SALARIES, WAGES, DIVIDENDS, INTEREST, ANNUITIES, AND FOR INCOMES FROM OTHER SOURCES REGARDLESS OF AMOUNTS

For Calendar Year 1940

or fiscal year beginning ________________, 1940, and ended ________________, 1941

To be filed with the Collector of Internal Revenue for your district not later than the 15th day of the third month following the close of your taxable year

PRINT NAME AND ADDRESS PLAINLY. (See Instruction C)

(Name) (Use given names of both husband and wife, if this is a joint return)

(Street and number, or rural route)

(Post office) (County) (State)

(Do not use these spaces)

File Code

Serial No.

District

(Cashier's Stamp)

Cash—Check—M. O.

First Payment

$

Item and Instruction No.

INCOME

1. Salaries and other compensation for personal services. (From Schedule A) $
2. Dividends
3. Interest on bank deposits, notes, mortgages, etc.
4. Interest on corporation bonds
5. Taxable interest on Government obligations, etc. (From Schedule B)
6. Income (or loss) from partnerships, syndicates, pools, etc. (other than capital gains or losses). (Furnish names and addresses):
7. Income from fiduciaries. (Furnish names and addresses):
8. Rents and royalties. (From Schedule C)
9. Income (or loss) from business or profession. (From Schedule D)
10. (*a*) Net short-term gain from sale or exchange of capital assets. (From Schedule F)
(*b*) Net long-term gain (or loss) from sale or exchange of capital assets. (From Schedule F)
(*c*) Net gain (or loss) from sale or exchange of property other than capital assets. (From Schedule G)
11. Other income (including income from annuities). (State nature)
12. Total income in items 1 to 11. (Enter nontaxable income in Schedule I) $

DEDUCTIONS

13. Contributions paid. (Explain in Schedule H) $
14. Interest. (Explain in Schedule H)
15. Taxes. (Explain in Schedule H)
16. Losses from fire, storm, shipwreck, or other casualty, or theft. (Explain in Schedule H)
17. Bad debts. (Explain in Schedule H)
18. Other deductions authorized by law. (Explain in Schedule H)
19. Total deductions in items 13 to 18
20. Net income (item 12 minus item 19) $

COMPUTATION OF TAX

21. Net income (item 20 above) $
22. Less: Personal exemption. (Explain in Schedule J-1) $
23. Credit for dependents. (Explain in Schedule J-2)
24. Balance (surtax net income) $
25. Less: Interest on Government obligations, etc. (See Instruction 25) $
26. Earned income credit. (From Schedule K-1 or K-2)
27. Balance subject to normal tax $
28. Normal tax (4% of item 27) $
29. Surtax on item 24. (See Instruction 29)
30. Total (item 28 plus item 29) $
31. Total income tax (item 30, or if you had a net long-term capital gain or loss, enter line 16, Schedule F) $
32. Less: (Income tax paid at source) $
33. Income tax paid to a foreign country or U.S. possession. (Attach Form 1116)
34. Balance of income tax (item 31 minus items 32 and 33) $
35. Defense tax (10% of item 31). (See Instruction 35)
36. Total income and defense taxes due (item 34 plus item 35) $

NOTE.—In order that this return my be accepted as meeting the requirements of the Internal Revenue Code, the data called for herein must be set forth FULLY and CLEARLY.

16—17104

FORM 1040
U.S. Treasury Department
Internal Revenue Service

U. S. INDIVIDUAL INCOME TAX RETURN

1950
CALENDAR YEAR

For other taxable years ending after Sept. 30, 1950, but before Dec. 31, 1951, attach Form 1040FY

Do not write in these spaces

Serial No.

(Cashier's Stamp)

EMPLOYEES: Instead of this form, you may use Form 1040A if your total income was less than $5,000, consisting wholly of wages shown on Forms W-2, or of such wages and not more than $100 of other wages, dividends, and interest.

Name ______________________________
(PLEASE PRINT. If this is a joint return of husband and wife, use first names of both)

HOME ADDRESS ______________________________
(PLEASE PRINT. Street and number or rural route)

____
(City, town, or post office) (Postal zone number) (State)

Social Security No. ______________ Occupation ______________

Your exemptions

1. **List your own name.**
If married and your wife (or husband) had no income, or if this is a joint return of husband and wife, list name of your wife (or husband).

List names of other close relatives (as defined in instructions) with 1950 gross incomes of less than $500 who received more than one-half of their support from you in 1950. If this is a joint return of husband and wife, list dependent relatives of both.

Name (please print)	Check below whether you (or your wife) were at the end of your taxable year— 65 OR OVER	BLIND	On lines a and b below Write 1 if neither 65 nor blind; Write 2 if either 65 or blind; Write 3 if both 65 and blind.
Your name ______________	Yes ☐ No ☐	Yes ☐ No ☐	a. Number of exemptions for you ______
Wife's (or husband's) name ______________	Yes ☐ No ☐	Yes ☐ No ☐	b. Number of her (his) exemptions ______

Name of Other Dependent Relative	Relationship	Address—if different from yours

Enter here total number of exemptions claimed (yours and your wife's plus one for each dependent listed above) ⟶

Your income

2. **Enter your total wages, salaries, bonuses, commissions, and other compensation received in 1950, BEFORE PAY-ROLL DEDUCTIONS for taxes, dues, insurance, bonds, etc. Also enter amount of income tax withheld. Members of Armed Forces and persons claiming traveling or reimbursed expenses, see instructions.**

Print Employer's Name	Where Employed (City and State)	Amount of Income Tax Withheld	Total Wages
		$	$
	Enter totals	$	$

3. If you received dividends, interest, or any other income, give details on page 2 and enter the total here ______

4. Add income shown in items 2 and 3, and enter total here ______ $

How to figure the tax

IF YOUR INCOME WAS LESS THAN $5,000.—Use the table on page 4 to find your tax—unless you itemize your deductions. This table allows about 10 percent of your total income for charitable contributions, interest, taxes, medical expenses, etc. If such deductions exceed 10 percent, it will usually be to your advantage to itemize them and compute your tax on page 3.

IF INCOME WAS $5,000 OR MORE.—Do not use tax table. Compute tax on page 3. Use standard deduction or itemize deductions, whichever is to your advantage.
HUSBAND AND WIFE.—For split-income benefits, file a joint return. If filing separate returns, and one itemizes deductions, both must itemize.

Tax due or refund

5. Enter your tax from table on page 4, or from line 18, page 3 ______ $

6. How much have you paid on your 1950 income tax?
(A) By tax withheld (in item 2, above). Attach Original Forms W-2 ______ $
(B) By payments on 1950 Declaration of Estimated Tax ______
Enter total here ⟶

7. If your tax (item 5) is larger than payments (item 6), enter **BALANCE OF TAX DUE** here ______ $
This balance of tax due must be paid in full with return.

8. If your payments (item 6) are larger than your tax (item 5), enter the **OVERPAYMENT** here ______ $
Enter amount of item 8 you want: Refunded to you $______; Credited on your 1951 estimated tax $______
Do you owe any prior year Federal tax for which you have been billed? ______ (Yes or No)

If you filed a return for a prior year, state latest year ______
Where filed ______
To which Collector's office did you pay amount claimed in item 6 (B), above? ______

County in which you reside ______
Is your wife (or husband) making a separate return for 1950? ______ (Yes or No)
If "Yes," write her (or his) name ______

I declare under the penalties of perjury that this return (including any accompanying schedules and statements) has been examined by me and to the best of my knowledge and belief is a true, correct, and complete return.

______ (Signature of person, other than taxpayer, preparing this return) ______ (Date)

______ (Signature of taxpayer) ______ (Date)

______ (Name of firm or employer, if any)

______ (Signature of taxpayer's wife or husband if this is a joint return) ______ (Date)

To assure any benefits of split-income provisions, husband and wife must include all their income, and BOTH MUST SIGN, even though only one has income.

● ATTACH CHECK OR MONEY ORDER HERE ● ATTACH COPY B OF FORMS W-2 HERE ●

FORM **1040**

U.S. Treasury Department
Internal Revenue Service

U.S. INDIVIDUAL INCOME TAX RETURN—1960

or Other Taxable Year Beginning ...., 1960, Ending ...., 19......

PLEASE PRINT OR TYPE

First name and initial | **Last name**

(If this is a joint return of husband and wife, use first names and middle initials of both)

Home address .... (Number and street or rural route)

(City, town, or post office) (Postal zone number) (State)

Your Social Security Number	Occupation	Wife's Social Security Number	Occupation

Exemptions

1. Check blocks which apply. Check for wife only if all of her income is included in this return, or if she had no income.
   - (a) Regular $600 exemption .... ☐ Yourself ☐ Wife
   - (b) Additional $600 exemption if 65 or over at end of taxable year. ☐ Yourself ☐ Wife
   - (c) Additional $600 exemption if blind at end of taxable year..... ☐ Yourself ☐ Wife

   Enter number of exemptions checked →

2. List first names of your children who qualify as dependents; ***give address if different from yours.*** **Enter number of children listed** →
3. Enter number of exemptions claimed for other persons listed at top of page 2 ....
4. Enter the total number of exemptions claimed on lines 1, 2, and 3 ....

Income

5. Enter all wages, salaries, bonuses, commissions, tips, and other compensation before payroll deductions (including any excess of expense account or similar allowance paid by your employer over your ordinary and necessary business expenses. See instructions, pp. 5-6.)

Employer's Name	Where Employed (City and State)	(a) Wages, etc.	(b) Federal Income Tax Withheld
		$	$
	Enter totals here →	$	$

6. Less: Excludable "Sick Pay" in line 5 (See instructions, page 7. Attach required statement.) ...
7. Balance (line 5 less line 6) .... $
8. Profit (or loss) from business from separate Schedule C .... ♦
9. Profit (or loss) from farming from separate Schedule F .... ♦
10. Other income (or loss) from page 3 (**Dividends, Interest, Rents, Pensions, etc.**)
11. Adjusted Gross Income (sum of lines 7, 8, 9, and 10) .... ▲ $

If the social security tax (FICA) withheld from wages exceeded $144 because you or your wife had more than one employer, see instructions, page 5.

● **Check if unmarried "Head of Household" ☐, or "Surviving Widow or Widower" with dependent child ☐. (See Instructions pp. 7-8)**

Tax due or refund

12. TAX on income on line 11. (If line 11 is under $5,000, and you do not itemize deductions, use Tax Table on page 16 of instructions to find your tax and check here ☐. If line 11 is $5,000 or more, or if you itemize deductions, compute your tax on page 2 and enter here the amount from line 9, page 2). $

If income was all from wages, omit lines 13 through 16

13. (a) Dividends received credit from line 5 of Schedule J ...... $
    (b) Retirement income credit from line 12 of Schedule K ....
14. Balance (line 12 less line 13) .... $
15. Enter your self-employment tax from separate Schedule C or F ....
16. Sum of lines 14 and 15 .... $
17. (a) Federal tax withheld (line 5, col. (b) above). Attach Forms W-2, Copy B .. $
    (b) Payments and credits on 1960 Declaration of Estimated Tax (See page 8, instructions.) ● $
    District Director's office where paid ....
18. If your tax (line 12 or 16) is larger than your payments (line 17), enter the BALANCE DUE here → $
    Pay in full with this return to "Internal Revenue Service." If less than $1.00, file return without payment.
19. If your payments (line 17) are larger than your tax (line 12 or 16), enter the OVERPAYMENT here → $
    If less than $1.00, the overpayment will be refunded only upon application.
20. Amount of line 19 to be: (a) Credited on 1961 estimated tax $.......... ; (b) Refunded $..........

Did you receive an expense allowance or reimbursement, or charge expenses to your employer? ☐ Yes ☐ No
If "Yes," did you submit an itemized accounting of expenses to your employer? .... ☐ Yes ☐ No
(See page 6, instructions.)

County in which you live.	Is your wife (husband) filing a separate return for 1960? ☐ Yes ☐ No. If "yes," enter her (his) name and do not claim the exemption on this return.	Do you owe any Federal tax for years before 1960? ☐ Yes ☐ No. If "Yes," enter here the Internal Revenue District where the account is outstanding.

I declare under the penalties of perjury that this return (including any accompanying schedules and statements) has been examined by me and to the best of my knowledge and belief is a true, correct, and complete return. If the return is prepared by a person other than the taxpayer, his declaration is based on all the information relating to the matters required to be reported in the return of which he has any knowledge.

Sign here ....

(Taxpayer's signature and date) (If this is a joint return, BOTH HUSBAND AND WIFE MUST SIGN) (Wife's signature and date)

(Signature of preparer other than taxpayer) (Address) (Date)

c70--16—76136-1

Form **1040** US Department of the Treasury / Internal Revenue Service

Individual Income Tax Return 1970

For the year January 1–December 31, 1970, or other taxable year beginning ...., 1970, ending ...., 19....

Please print or type

First name and initial (If joint return, use first names and middle initials of both)	Last name	Your social security number
Present home address (Number and street or rural route)		Spouse's social security number
City, town or post office, State and ZIP code		Occupation: Yours / Spouse's

Filing Status—check only one:

1 ☐ Single; 2 ☐ Married filing jointly (even if only one had income)

3 ☐ Married filing separately and spouse is also filing. If this item checked give spouse's social security number in space above and enter first name here ▶

4 ☐ Unmarried Head of Household

5 ☐ Surviving widow(er) with dependent child

6 ☐ Married filing separately and spouse is not filing

Exemptions Regular / 65 or over / Blind — Enter number of boxes checked ▶

7 Yourself . . . . ☐ ☐ ☐

8 Spouse (applies only if item 2 or 6 is checked) ☐ ☐ ☐

9 First names of your dependent children who lived with you .... Enter number ▶

10 Number of other dependents (from line 34) . . . ▶

11 Total exemptions claimed . . . . ▶

Please attach Copy B of Form W–2 to back

Income

12 Wages, salaries, tips, etc. (Attach Forms W–2 to back. If unavailable, attach explanation) . | 12

13a Dividends (see pages 5 and 9 of instr.) $........ 13b Less exclusion $........ Balance . ▶ | 13c

(Also list in Part I of Schedule B, if gross dividends and other distributions are over $100)

14 Interest. Enter total here (also list in Part II of Schedule B, if total is over $100) . . . | 14

15 Income other than wages, dividends, and interest (from line 40) . . . . | 15

16 Total (add lines 12, 13c, 14 and 15) . . . . | 16

17 Adjustments to income (such as "sick pay," moving expense, etc. from line 45) . . . | 17

18 Adjusted gross income (subtract line 17 from line 16) . . . . | 18

- *See page 2 of instructions for rules under which the IRS will figure your tax and surcharge.*
- *If you do not itemize deductions and line 18 is under $10,000, find tax in Tables. Enter tax on line 19.*
- *If you itemize deductions or line 18 is $10,000 or more, go to line 46 to figure tax.*

Tax and Surcharge

19 Tax (Check if from: Tax Tables 1–15 ☐, Tax Rate Schedule X, Y, or Z ☐, Schedule D ☐, or Schedule G ☐) | 19

20 Tax surcharge. See Tax Surcharge Tables A, B and C in instructions. (If you claim retirement income credit, use Schedule R to figure surcharge.) . . . . | 20

21 Total (add lines 19 and 20) . . . . | 21

Please attach Check or Money Order here

Payments and Credits

22 Total credits (from line 55) . . . . | 22

23 Income tax (subtract line 22 from line 21) . . . . | 23

24 Other taxes (from line 61) . . . . | 24

25 Total (add lines 23 and 24) . . . . | 25

26 Total Federal income tax withheld (attach Forms W–2 to back) . | 26

27 1970 Estimated tax payments (include 1969 overpayment allowed as a credit) | 27

28 Other payments (from line 65) . . . . | 28

Make check or money order payable to Internal Revenue Service.

29 Total (add lines 26, 27, and 28) . . . . | 29

Bal. Due or Refund

30 If line 25 is larger than line 29, enter BALANCE DUE. Pay in full with return . . . ▶ | 30

31 If line 29 is larger than line 25, enter OVERPAYMENT . . . . ▶ | 31

32 Line 31 to be: (a) Credited on 1971 estimated tax ▶ $ .... ; (b) Refunded ▶ $

Under penalties of perjury, I declare that I have examined this return, including accompanying schedules and statements, and to the best of my knowledge and belief it is true, correct, and complete.

Sign here

Your signature .... Date ....

Signature of preparer other than taxpayer, based on all information of which he has any knowledge. .... Date ....

Spouse's signature (if filing jointly, BOTH must sign even if only one had income) ....

Address ....

16—81168–1

Form **1040** Department of the Treasury—Internal Revenue Service
U.S. Individual Income Tax Return 1980

For Privacy Act Notice, see Instructions | For the year January 1–December 31, 1980, or other tax year beginning 1980, ending 19

Use IRS label. Otherwise, please print or type.

- Your first name and initial (if joint return, also give spouse's name and initial) — Last name — Your social security number
- Present home address (Number and street, including apartment number, or rural route) — Spouse's social security no.
- City, town or post office, State and ZIP code — Your occupation ▶ — Spouse's occupation ▶

Presidential Election Campaign Fund ▶ Do you want $1 to go to this fund? . . . . Yes No
If joint return, does your spouse want $1 to go to this fund? . . . Yes No
Note: *Checking "Yes" will not increase your tax or reduce your refund.*

Requested by Census Bureau for Revenue Sharing ▶
A Where do you live (actual location of residence)? (See page 2 of Instructions.) State | City, village, borough, etc.
B Do you live within the legal limits of a city, village, etc.? ☐ Yes ☐ No
C In what county do you live?
D In what township do you live?

Filing Status

Check only one box.

For IRS use only

1 Single
2 Married filing joint return (even if only one had income)
3 Married filing separate return. Enter spouse's social security no. above and full name here ▶
4 Head of household. (See page 6 of Instructions.) If qualifying person is your unmarried child, enter child's name ▶
5 Qualifying widow(er) with dependent child (Year spouse died ▶ 19). (See page 6 of Instructions.)

Exemptions

Always check the box labeled Yourself. Check other boxes if they apply.

6a Yourself — 65 or over — Blind
b Spouse — 65 or over — Blind
Enter number of boxes checked on 6a and b ▶

c First names of your dependent children who lived with you ▶
Enter number of children listed on 6c ▶

d Other dependents:

(1) Name	(2) Relationship	(3) Number of months lived in your home	(4) Did dependent have income of $1,000 or more?	(5) Did you provide more than one-half of dependent's support?

Enter number of other dependents ▶

7 Total number of exemptions claimed . . . . Add numbers entered in boxes above ▶

Income

Please attach Copy B of your Forms W–2 here.

If you do not have a W-2, see page 5 of Instructions.

Please attach check or money order here.

8 Wages, salaries, tips, etc. 8
9 Interest income *(attach Schedule B if over $400)* 9
10a Dividends *(attach Schedule B if over $400)* ______, 10b Exclusion ______
c Subtract line 10b from line 10a 10c
11 Refunds of State and local income taxes *(do not enter an amount unless you deducted those taxes in an earlier year—see page 9 of Instructions)* 11
12 Alimony received 12
13 Business income or (loss) *(attach Schedule C)* 13
14 Capital gain or (loss) *(attach Schedule D)* 14
15 40% of capital gain distributions not reported on line 14 (See page 9 of Instructions) . 15
16 Supplemental gains or (losses) *(attach Form 4797)* 16
17 Fully taxable pensions and annuities not reported on line 18 17
18 Pensions, annuities, rents, royalties, partnerships, etc. *(attach Schedule E)* 18
19 Farm income or (loss) *(attach Schedule F)* 19
20a Unemployment compensation (insurance). Total received ______
b Taxable amount, if any, from worksheet on page 10 of Instructions 20b
21 Other income (state nature and source—see page 10 of Instructions) ▶ ______ 21
22 **Total income.** Add amounts in column for lines 8 through 21 . . . . ▶ 22

Adjustments to Income

(See Instructions on page 10)

23 Moving expense *(attach Form 3903 or 3903F)* 23
24 Employee business expenses *(attach Form 2106)* . . 24
25 Payments to an IRA (enter code from page 10 ......) . 25
26 Payments to a Keogh *(H.R. 10)* retirement plan . . . 26
27 Interest penalty on early withdrawal of savings . . . 27
28 Alimony paid 28
29 Disability income exclusion *(attach Form 2440)* . . . 29
30 **Total adjustments.** Add lines 23 through 29 . . . . ▶ 30

Adjusted Gross Income

31 **Adjusted gross income.** Subtract line 30 from line 22. *If this line is less than $10,000, see "Earned Income Credit" (line 57) on pages 13 and 14 of Instructions. If you want IRS to figure your tax, see page 3 of Instructions* . . . . ▶ 31

Form **1040** Department of the Treasury—Internal Revenue Service

U.S. Individual Income Tax Return **1990** (0)

For the year Jan.–Dec. 31, 1990, or other tax year beginning , 1990, ending 19 OMB No. 1545-0074

Label (See Instructions on page 8.)

Use IRS label. Otherwise, please print or type.

LABEL HERE

Your first name and initial	Last name	Your social security number
If a joint return, spouse's first name and initial	Last name	Spouse's social security number
Home address (number and street) (If you have a P.O. box, see page 9.)	Apt. no.	**For Privacy Act and Paperwork Reduction Act Notice, see Instructions.**
City, town or post office, state, and ZIP code. (If you have a foreign address, see page 9.)		

Presidential Election Campaign (See page 9.)

Do you want $1 to go to this fund?	Yes	No	**Note:** *Checking "Yes" will not change your tax or reduce your refund.*
If joint return, does your spouse want $1 to go to this fund?	Yes	No	

Filing Status

Check only one box.

1 Single. (See page 10 to find out if you can file as head of household.)
2 Married filing joint return (even if only one had income)
3 Married filing separate return. Enter spouse's social security no. above and full name here. ▶
4 Head of household (with qualifying person). (See page 10.) If the qualifying person is your child but not your dependent, enter this child's name here. ▶
5 Qualifying widow(er) with dependent child (year spouse died ▶ 19). (See page 10.)

Exemptions

(See Instructions on page 10.)

6a ☐ **Yourself** If your parent (or someone else) can claim you as a dependent on his or her tax return, do not check box 6a. But be sure to check the box on line 33b on page 2

b ☐ **Spouse**

No. of boxes checked on 6a and 6b ____

c **Dependents:**

(1) Name (first, initial, and last name)	(2) Check if under age 2	(3) If age 2 or older, dependent's social security number	(4) Dependent's relationship to you	(5) No. of months lived in your home in 1990

No. of your children on 6c who:
- lived with you ____
- didn't live with you due to divorce or separation (see page 11) ____

No. of other dependents on 6c ____

If more than 6 dependents, see Instructions on page 11.

d If your child didn't live with you but is claimed as your dependent under a pre-1985 agreement, check here ▶ ☐

e Total number of exemptions claimed . . . . Add numbers entered on lines above ▶ ☐

Income

Attach Copy B of your Forms W-2, W-2G, and W-2P here

If you do not have a W-2, see page 8.

Attach check or money order on top of any Forms W-2, W-2G, or W-2P.

7	Wages, salaries, tips, etc. *(attach Form(s) W-2)*		7
8a	**Taxable** interest income *(also attach Schedule B if over $400)*		8a
b	**Tax-exempt** interest income (see page 13). DON'T include on line 8a	8b	
9	Dividend income *(also attach Schedule B if over $400)*		9
10	Taxable refunds of state and local income taxes, if any, from worksheet on page 14		10
11	Alimony received		11
12	Business income or (loss) *(attach Schedule C)*		12
13	Capital gain or (loss) *(attach Schedule D)*		13
14	Capital gain distributions not reported on line 13 (see page 14)		14
15	Other gains or (losses) *(attach Form 4797)*		15
16a	Total IRA distributions	16a	16b Taxable amount (see page 14) 16b
17a	Total pensions and annuities	17a	17b Taxable amount (see page 14) 17b
18	Rents, royalties, partnerships, estates, trusts, etc. *(attach Schedule E)*		18
19	Farm income or (loss) *(attach Schedule F)*		19
20	Unemployment compensation (insurance) (see page 16)		20
21a	Social security benefits	21a	21b Taxable amount (see page 16) 21b
22	Other income (list type and amount—see page 16)		22
23	Add the amounts shown in the far right column for lines 7 through 22. This is your **total income** ▶		23

Adjustments to Income

(See Instructions on page 17.)

24a	Your IRA deduction, from applicable worksheet on page 17 or 18	24a	
b	Spouse's IRA deduction, from applicable worksheet on page 17 or 18	24b	
25	One-half of self-employment tax (see page 18)	25	
26	Self-employed health insurance deduction, from worksheet on page 18	26	
27	Keogh retirement plan and self-employed SEP deduction	27	
28	Penalty on early withdrawal of savings	28	
29	Alimony paid. Recipient's SSN ▶	29	
30	Add lines 24a through 29. These are your **total adjustments** ▶		30

Adjusted Gross Income

31	Subtract line 30 from line 23. This is your **adjusted gross income.** *If this amount is less than $20,264 and a child lived with you, see page 23 to find out if you can claim the "Earned Income Credit" on line 57* ▶	31

Form **1040** Department of the Treasury—Internal Revenue Service

U.S. Individual Income Tax Return 2000

(99) IRS Use Only—Do not write or staple in this space.

For the year Jan. 1–Dec. 31, 2000, or other tax year beginning , 2000, ending , 20 OMB No. 1545-0074

Label (See instructions on page 19.) **Use the IRS label.** Otherwise, please print or type.

LABEL HERE

Your first name and initial	Last name
If a joint return, spouse's first name and initial	Last name
Home address (number and street). If you have a P.O. box, see page 19.	Apt. no.
City, town or post office, state, and ZIP code. If you have a foreign address, see page 19.	

Your social security number

Spouse's social security number

▲ **Important!** ▲ You **must** enter your SSN(s) above.

Presidential Election Campaign (See page 19.)

Note. Checking "Yes" will not change your tax or reduce your refund.
Do you, or your spouse if filing a joint return, want $3 to go to this fund? ▶ You ☐ Yes ☐ No Spouse ☐ Yes ☐ No

Filing Status

Check only one box.

1 ☐ Single
2 ☐ Married filing joint return (even if only one had income)
3 ☐ Married filing separate return. Enter spouse's social security no. above and full name here. ▶
4 ☐ Head of household (with qualifying person). (See page 19.) If the qualifying person is a child but not your dependent, enter this child's name here. ▶
5 ☐ Qualifying widow(er) with dependent child (year spouse died ▶). (See page 19.)

Exemptions

6a ☐ **Yourself.** If your parent (or someone else) can claim you as a dependent on his or her tax return, **do not** check box 6a

b ☐ **Spouse**

c **Dependents:**

(1) First name Last name	(2) Dependent's social security number	(3) Dependent's relationship to you	(4) ✓ if qualifying child for child tax credit (see page 20)
			☐
			☐
			☐
			☐
			☐
			☐

If more than six dependents, see page 20.

d Total number of exemptions claimed

No. of boxes checked on 6a and 6b
No. of your children on 6c who:
• lived with you
• did not live with you due to divorce or separation (see page 20)
Dependents on 6c not entered above
Add numbers entered on lines above ▶

Income

Attach Forms W-2 and W-2G here. Also attach Form(s) 1099-R if tax was withheld.

If you did not get a W-2, see page 21.

Enclose, but do not attach, any payment. Also, please use **Form 1040-V.**

7	Wages, salaries, tips, etc. Attach Form(s) W-2	7	
8a	**Taxable** interest. Attach Schedule B if required	8a	
b	**Tax-exempt** interest. **Do not** include on line 8a 8b		
9	Ordinary dividends. Attach Schedule B if required	9	
10	Taxable refunds, credits, or offsets of state and local income taxes (see page 22)	10	
11	Alimony received	11	
12	Business income or (loss). Attach Schedule C or C-EZ	12	
13	Capital gain or (loss). Attach Schedule D if required. If not required, check here ▶ ☐	13	
14	Other gains or (losses). Attach Form 4797	14	
15a	Total IRA distributions 15a b Taxable amount (see page 23)	15b	
16a	Total pensions and annuities 16a b Taxable amount (see page 23)	16b	
17	Rental real estate, royalties, partnerships, S corporations, trusts, etc. Attach Schedule E	17	
18	Farm income or (loss). Attach Schedule F	18	
19	Unemployment compensation	19	
20a	Social security benefits 20a b Taxable amount (see page 25)	20b	
21	Other income. List type and amount (see page 25)	21	
22	Add the amounts in the far right column for lines 7 through 21. This is your **total income** ▶	22	

Adjusted Gross Income

23	IRA deduction (see page 27)	23	
24	Student loan interest deduction (see page 27)	24	
25	Medical savings account deduction. Attach Form 8853	25	
26	Moving expenses. Attach Form 3903	26	
27	One-half of self-employment tax. Attach Schedule SE	27	
28	Self-employed health insurance deduction (see page 29)	28	
29	Self-employed SEP, SIMPLE, and qualified plans	29	
30	Penalty on early withdrawal of savings	30	
31a	Alimony paid b Recipient's SSN ▶	31a	
32	Add lines 23 through 31a	32	
33	Subtract line 32 from line 22. This is your **adjusted gross income** ▶	33	

www.ingramcontent.com/pod-product-compliance
Lightning Source LLC
Chambersburg PA
CBHW040231220526
45473CB00001B/196

* 9 7 8 1 9 8 3 6 2 3 5 5 4 *